JUSTICE REFRAMED

How the Cross Confronts our Pursuit of Justice

By Tina Webb and Christopher Webb

Independent Author Publishing

Psalm 89:14-15

Righteousness and justice *are* the foundation of Your throne;
Mercy and truth go before Your face.
Blessed *are* the people who know the joyful sound!
They walk, O Lord, in the light of Your countenance.

Contents

Introduction

To truly see justice as God does, as believers, we study the Scriptures. Our understanding deepens, and our consciences are pricked as each of us realizes that His ways are not our ways, His thoughts are not our thoughts. We then wrestle with God, driven by our personal views and experiences with injustice. At some point, we lay on the ground like Jacob, knowing that our grappling has produced a greater dependence on our Creator. He cares when any member of this created race of human beings feels the pain of injustice or is the perpetrator of injustice. From this foundation, recognizing that justice is the by-product of God's care, we can view our actions and inspect our formed opinions. Only then will we know how to discern and address the injustice around us.

1

Leave Our Pride at the Cross

Many of you have this book in your hands because you are curious about what a young black man has to say about injustice. Or what does his black mother, who has three more sons, have to share? Through the years, my husband, our adult children, and I have wrestled with fears, carried righteous anger, and worked to keep an unoffended heart. It has not been easy.

But God is faithful, and he has directed us repeatedly to his Word, which not only reflects his divine will but his parental heart. I (Tina) have had to review how my lens was shaped—the settings and social circles that have influenced me. My experience with racism, which I prefer to call skin color bias (we are one human race) is few and far between compared to many people of color. So, I had to imagine the life experiences of people like my husband and realize the legitimacy of their pain, distrust, and anger. I looked into my husband's eyes as he told the story of being told to lay on the ground by a white cop in downtown Philadelphia. Doug had done nothing wrong but thought he would never see his mother again. I had to recall how I felt the two times I encountered people's prejudices. I was shocked. Angry. Offended. The first time I was followed around a retail store, and the second I was blatantly ignored by the white cashier. My white companion was incensed and stood up for me. But I have *never* gone into those stores again.

Despite my limited experience with racial injustice, I remember looking at the beautiful brown shades of my four sons when they were little, realizing that they would get "the Talk" from dad, and they would get a talk from me. *When you walk down the street, stand up straight, don't slump. If someone calls you a bad name, remember that they are ignorant and blind. Your unseen enemy is using them to bring you down. Stay up where Christ reigns. Forgive them and pray for them.*

One of my favorite quotes is "I shall allow no man to belittle my soul by making me hate him" by Booker T. Washington. Doug and I raised our six children to be fixed in their identity in Christ. To view being a redeemed child of God as the most significant identifier that they have. When protests and violence due to racial injustice increased this year, we prayed that bitterness would not become anchored in their hearts. Or fear and hatred. We hoped that they would 1) acknowledge the injustice that at any moment they could be mistreated due to the color of their skin, 2) give this reality to Jesus, and 3) carry his demon-binding, people-loving, reconciling presence wherever they go.

Christopher and I decided to write this book in June 2020. In the middle of yet another conversation about racism—specifically Christians and a Christlike response to injustice, we felt a nudge to dig deeper into the Scriptures. To solidify what we believed or, if necessary, exchange it for a biblical perspective. This short book is a glimpse of some of what we have gleaned.

For those of you looking for our Bible-based views on voting, protests, running for local offices, or community healing, you will have to wait until the last chapter. First, we *must* bring to light the collage of Christian perspectives, emotion, and heart postures when it comes to injustice. Throughout this discussion, we reference the Bible stories and verses that have informed our views about injustice.

*****

We all sit in a different space. Our various experiences inform our reactions, motives, and viewpoints. To bridge our differences and become an undivided Church, we must remember that we *perceive* in part[1]. While 1 Cor. 13:9 references spiritual revelation, this truth applies to the world around us. None of us will ever have the whole perspective on any issue. Our vantage point of any situation is based on where we sit and what lens we use to look through. In my book, *Culture Changers: Understand the Roots of Brokenness and Help Heal Your Family and Community*, I wrote this:

---

[1] 1 Corinthians 13:9 Now our knowledge is partial and incomplete, and even the gift of prophecy reveals only part of the whole picture!
ginōskō – know, perceive, understand, Strong's Concordance G1097

"...lenses influence how I see everything around me. Similarly, how we view the world will dictate how we interpret experiences, issues, and ourselves."

When it comes to injustice, as Jesus followers, we must use the Bible as our lens; find out what God thinks and the consequences he requires.

While many people use the term *Christian* to describe themselves, Paul helps us to recognize genuine believers from others. In 1 Corinthians 11:16, the Apostle writes, "I hear that there are divisions among you. And I believe it in part, for there must be factions among you so that those who are genuine among you may be recognized." Ouch! This statement must have offended some who thought themselves genuine in their belief. While someone may indeed be born again[2], the Bible is clear that words and deeds are often a maturity indicator of *the fruit* of our faith in Jesus Christ.

Our genuineness or authenticity can reflect the depth of revelation we have received from the Word of God. Another verse reminds us that some born again believers are immature in their understanding of Scripture, and not quite ready for the meat of the Word of God[3]. No matter where one is in their faith journey, those whose *confession of faith confirms the birth, death, and resurrection of the sinless Jesus Christ of Nazareth, who paid the price of sin on*

---

[2] John 3:3 Jesus answered and said to him, "Truly, truly, I say to you, unless one is born again, he cannot see the kingdom of God." (NASB)

[3] Hebrews 5:13 For everyone who partakes only of milk is unskilled in the word of righteousness, for he is a babe. (NKJV)

the cross so that righteousness can be obtained—those are our audience.

Every Nation, Tribe, And Tongue

You will read this differently than the next person. Your age, your ethnicity, cultural experience, and even your denomination has given you specific filters from which you see and think. Within the context of your genetics, you have a *bent*[4] that God gave you.

None is better than the other. By ourselves, we insufficiently represent God or understand God because we will always default to our filters and our bent. So, we need each other. Also, God has given specific characteristics to every nation, tribe, and tongue. While these characteristics or expressions will be tainted by sin, you and I can look at fellow believers from every tribe or heritage to glean how each one reveals a part of God's essence. **It takes all of humanity, with its varying cultural expressions, to portray the fullness of an infinite God.**

The myths that describe the origins of different people groups reveal much about the implicit filters within our worldviews. Some myths feature a picture of the divine as powerful, authoritative, and distant from humankind. Others reveal deities that came alongside humanity, creating them in community and then partnering with them to teach how humans ought to function. One reveals a more top-down view of leadership, the other a more collaborative perspective. When

---

[4] Bent – the way each of us is wired, from personality to giftings and calling.

compared with Scripture, both accurately describe our relationship with God, as bondservants yet, co-laborers. However, holding one *over* another can influence whether we respond to a certain expression of leadership as good or bad. Our cultural, ethnic, and national identities give us a filter through which we discern and evaluate. These filters make it easy for us to gravitate to people with common backgrounds and agree more easily with believers with similar giftings and callings.

God created human beings in His image, male and female, to complement one another. Then God divided us through language, ethnicity, and regional identity. These become our foundational social circles. God is bigger than any one nation, tribe, and tongue; therefore, none can ever represent His full essence. When we look at brothers and sisters from different social circles and the way they interpret or relate to God, we discover another amazing facet of God—one that *our* social circle may not emphasize. Therefore, we must *listen* to each other. God's purpose for distinctions is to glorify Himself, but division glorifies Satan. To destroy the divisions that perpetuate racial and other types of injustice, we must gain insight from the Word of God.

Our Sin of Self-Righteousness

Jesus paid the penalty for our sin nature—death. However, every day we face natural consequences for the behaviors, attitudes, and thoughts that are still sinful. We still sin because at salvation, our mindsets were not automatically reset. The journey of sanctification involves reviewing our thoughts and opinions under the light of

Scripture and discarding what does not match up. Any lack of agreement with scriptural teaching is the reason why conversations about injustice can be the same in Christian circles as they are in non-Christian circles.

Repentance[5]and renouncing secular views involve a degree of humility that can be difficult to embrace where personal and group identity are concerned. Why? Because we embrace groupthink, not reject it. Often, our identifiers—skin color, denomination, or age—as well as our social circles, give us a sense of pride, which, in God's eyes, can become an idol. Death to self necessitates *submitting* our primary identifiers and foundation-forming social circles (and the filters they imparted to us) to the Lordship of Christ. This decision to lose our lives[6] helps us represent Christ more fully rather than obscuring him with our humanity. Jesus is not willing to share a platform with our preferred identifiers; neither does he want to be just another compartment in our lives. We must love him first and more than any other.

Within the Christian community, the debate on the issues of racism and justice is similar to the discussions in non faith-based circles. To honestly reckon with how tough it is for us to surrender the views we have formed, we can think about our conversations with fellow

---

[5] Changing one's mind about a matter

[6] Matthew 10:35-39 For I came to set a man against his father, and a daughter against her mother, and a daughter-in-law against her mother-in-law; [36] and a man's enemies will be the members of his household.

[37] "He who loves father or mother more than Me is not worthy of Me; and he who loves son or daughter more than Me is not worthy of Me. [38] And he who does not take his cross and follow after Me is not worthy of Me. [39] He who has found his life will lose it, and he who has lost his life for My sake will find it.

believers about politics or morality. When was the last time you talked with another believer about prejudice? Gender identity? Was there a moment where the Spirit of God challenged you to rethink your view? Many of us don't engage in these conversations, and the reasons vary. A subtle reason is that diving into these discussions causes our dirty laundry to be too visible—too *in our face* for our comfort. Although, as Christians, we readily acknowledge our denominational differences, we have not been ready to admit that our division goes much deeper. External topics reveal a troubling internal heart posture. We think *our* way is right even if we have not studied to find out what the Bible says about a topic. Cain killed his brother due to pride and holding onto his sense of right. God warned him that sin was near, but Cain would not surrender. What did Cain hold on to? His view of justice. It is time to admit that we have followed mainly in Cain's footsteps.

We have a heart problem on our hands. Here is an example. Many of us have fallen into a subconscious opinion that *our* way is best and closest to Jesus' ideal of how the Church should look, behave, and speak. To illustrate, let's look at our choice of a local church —why we choose one congregation over another. We call our choice, *preference*, yet politely distance ourselves from Christians who prefer a style of worship that is different— or whose church membership looks different than what we are accustomed to. Sunday morning has historically been the most racially divided time of day. However, preference and comfort become prejudice when we subconsciously look down upon people with whom we are going to spend eternity. I wonder what the Baptist is going to say when he realizes that his heavenly neighbor was a Prosperity Preacher that he spoke against. Our manner—our message is dictated too much by our judgment of others and not enough by the Word of God. It is time to let God break up the fallow ground of our hearts.

Consider the debates that center around social justice and poverty. Who is right, those who hold up a banner of personal responsibility or those who hold the position of compassion and altruism? Or what about what candidate to vote for? The one who everyone loves to hate—because of his elitist comments and brash personality? Or the one who crossed the racial barrier and gave a pass to issues that most Christians call sin? Politics has caused our self-righteous opinions to rise to the top. One of our greatest sins is inflating our opinions rather than running to our Bible to find out what God thinks about a topic and a person.

The Bride of Christ is divided. We are busy pointing fingers at one another. Let's ask God to inspect our hearts to show us any mindset that is not aligned with His. It is time to ask Him, "Lord, which of my preferences have crossed over to prejudice?"

As Christians, we are the ones that have a relationship with the ultimate Problem-solver. We can allow the sum of Word to guide our opinions and highlight our hypocrisies. We must learn to listen to our circles of influences and recognize when their filters are Biblically inaccurate. Recently, I had to repent for giving more time and attention to social media debates about the demolition of statues than opening my Bible to find God's opinion. I began to do a word study on memorial stones, stones of remembrance, and idols. The Bible must be the foundation on which we stand on an issue.

Enthroning our preferences or prejudices causes us to miss the heart of God and fall into judgementalism. *Why do those protesters have to be so loud?* Many of us have seen the pictures of white police officers and black Christians washing one another's feet. *That gesture surely couldn't be sincere.* But what does God think?

As Christ-followers, we have to acknowledge where our manner and our message has not reflected His. We have to see how we have seared our consciences through self-righteousness, which has widened the very gaps we are called to close.

The Bible Is Still Relevant

For some, Sunday morning pulpits have historically been the platforms of the town crier--the prophetic voice calling for repentance and change in the public square. Yet, how many of the listeners stay ignorant of the totality of God's view on a topic? We need to hear the rallying cry, yet we need a observe how Jesus deals with societal issues. It is interesting to find that Jesus never instructed the Jews to rise up against the Romans. He never called for an overt protest against oppression. Paul's appeal to the Jews to be in subjection to civil leaders—even unjust ones confound many of us.   When Peter cut the soldier's ear off with a sword, Jesus rebuked him.

Throughout the Old Testament, we read that God will avenge and defend the poor and oppressed. However,

Jesus and the apostles do not execute God's vengeance in the way we expect or desire. The way God punishes evildoers carries the goal of reconciliation, not retaliation or banishment. How many of today's marginalized are looking to reconcile with police officers, racist Americans, or other oppressors? (Or vice versa)

The Bible has not always been referenced in conversations about racial injustice these past several months. I wonder if many of us don't integrate faith and social issues. I also wonder how well we are equipped to identify faulty filters or biases? For example, when was the last time you heard your pastor urge the congregation to take the beam from their eyes before pointing out the log in someone's eyes? Scripture reveals that none of us see clearly; rather, we have to deal with ourselves first. How often do we talk about the verse 'love your enemies' in our like-minded circles? I (Tina) find that a more significant error has been to group humanity together as one entity. God never expects sinners to do what only saints have the ability in Christ to do. When we join in public discourse and ignore the fact that some in the conversation are carnally minded[7], we do ourselves and

---

[7] Romans 8:5-9 For those who are according to the flesh set their minds on the things of the flesh, but those who are according to the Spirit, the things of the Spirit. [6] For the mind set on the flesh is death, but the mind set on the Spirit is life and peace, [7] because the mind set on the flesh is hostile toward God; for it does not subject itself to the law of God, for it is not even able to do so, [8] and those who are in the flesh cannot please God. [9] However, you are not in the flesh but in the Spirit, if indeed the Spirit of God dwells in you. But if anyone does not have the Spirit of Christ, he does not belong to Him. (NASB)

Ephesians 4:18 - Being darkened in their under-standing, excluded from the life of God because of the ignorance that is in them, because of the hardness of their heart; (NASB)

them a disservice. We enter the conversation on their terms, and we end up either leaving God's lens out of the entire conversation or using the Bible as a prop only when we want it.

The recent events have prompted conversations about racial reconciliation, systemic racism, what true repentance looks like, and even the illegitimacy of the word "race" itself. Some believers have decided that "white guilt" is a reasonable scarlet letter. Or white privilege a needed admission. Many Christians are seeking to implement the solutions offered by ethnic minorities, like reviewing law enforcement practices or pursuing legal reparations for descendants of slaves. These external solutions have a place for debate in the public square; however, should we believe that the resolution of racial injustice will occur if these measures are passed? They cannot be because there will always be lawbreakers just as there will always be sinners.

Biblical Resolution Challenges Us

Some believers slough off the comments and topics that challenge us to take an in-depth look into our hearts and examine our reasoning for calling for justice. We think more about natural consequences than eternal forgiveness. Our stakes in the current arguments have become more tied to political loyalties and less based on our Biblical convictions. Why?

As the redeemed, we are the ones with the capacity to provide lasting solutions for any type of injustice. Our mission is to be front and center like Jesus was. His words and actions caught the attention of civil and religious leaders as well as the needy and the oppressed. Jesus' message collided with established doctrine and ideals. To follow his example, we must surrender all—viewpoints, doctrine, and ideals that have been formed by our social circles. Then we must agree to live with our hearts and minds under the microscope of the Bible.

God's light shines in the darkness and uncovers heart issues that we don't always like to face. For example, has it ever dawned on you that many things that are egregious to God are not only accepted in the Church but encouraged? We often don't give a second thought about slander, greed, or foul language. We "harass" our politicians and pastors when they commit adultery but don't hold ourselves to the biblical standard and embrace God's call for the holiness of the marriage covenant, sexual purity, and integrity. Yet these sins are ones that Paul urges the Colossian church to reject and turn from; he also reminds them that these sins were taken care of by Christ on the cross.

> So put to death the sinful, earthly things lurking within you. Have nothing to do with sexual immorality, impurity, lust, and evil desires. Don't be greedy, for a greedy person is an idolater, worshiping the things of this world. Because of these sins, the anger of God is coming. You used to do these things when your life was still part of this world. But now is the time to get rid of anger, rage, malicious behavior, slander, and dirty language. Don't lie to each other, for you have stripped off your old sinful nature and all its

wicked deeds. Put on your new nature and be renewed as you learn to know your Creator and become like him. In this new life, it doesn't matter if you are a Jew or a Gentile, circumcised or uncircumcised, barbaric, uncivilized, slave, or free. Christ is all that matters, and he lives in all of us.[8]

The above passage references 'the handwriting of requirements that was against us' (paraphrase). In the heavenly court of justice, where God sits as Judge, the enemy accuses us of our guilt. Always an accuser, the devil establishes his right to attack us when we sin. He is not wrong to do so. Guilt for a crime requires justice. His petition to God is for us to suffer the just consequences of our sins. Every possible sin breaks God's law in such a significant way that for human beings to be released from the penalty of sin and be reconciled as sons and daughters, God had to make atonement. His verdict was that he would be penalized for our crimes. As the eternal Judge, God took the consequence of the lawbreaker. Pretty heavy stuff. When we grapple with civil law, voice our accusations about someone else's conduct, and cry for

---

[8] Colossians 3:5-11 So put to death the sinful, earthly things lurking within you. Have nothing to do with sexual immorality, impurity, lust, and evil desires. Don't be greedy, for a greedy person is an idolater, worshiping the things of this world. [6] Because of these sins, the anger of God is coming. [7] You used to do these things when your life was still part of this world. [8] But now is the time to get rid of anger, rage, malicious behavior, slander, and dirty language. [9] Don't lie to each other, for you have stripped off your old sinful nature and all its wicked deeds. [10] Put on your new nature, and be renewed as you learn to know your Creator and become like him. [11] In this new life, it doesn't matter if you are a Jew or a Gentile, circumcised or uncircumcised, barbaric, uncivilized, slave, or free. Christ is all that matters, and he lives in all of us. (NLT)

consequences, how often do we allow God's posture towards the guilty to guide us?

Let's take this a step further. Not only are many of the transgressions of God's law unaccounted for by our civil government, but we have enacted laws that protect the right of people to do the exact opposite of what God commands. People are allowed to divorce for any reason under the sun. Or get an abortion. Yet prayer, worship, and reading the Bible are not allowed in the public school systems or some public places. By law, our society's position on marriage, already referenced above, is in direct contradiction to what God established in the first two chapters of Genesis.

Questions

- Read Matthew 22:21. If Jesus' implication is that God's law and property supersede that of civil government, in what ways should our governmental system and laws change?

- As Christians, how do we hold God's law in the highest regard while respecting ungodly civil laws?

In terms of how we respond to or legislate injustice, we cannot use human law and precedent as the standard because they are not always an accurate representation of God's ways. We must hold ourselves to what is considered right and just in heaven's court and halls of justice. Then we use *that* to inform our responses to what happens within our society and civil government. The world will cry for consequences that they deem reasonable, but we, followers of Christ, are accountable to God.

If we are honest, many of us care less about the spiritual consequences of injustice than the civil consequences. However, we are called to represent Christ, not a human version of justice. We are called to separate ourselves from the world's thinking and to represent God's life and ways in how we respond to the injustice and brokenness of our world.

Jesus Offends All of Us at Times

During his ministry of reconciliation, Jesus' authority and teachings were an offense to some, yet a breath of fresh air to others. Why?

Truth sometimes meets stubbornness and pride. All of us are guilty. Our heart gets hardened, and our minds stay comfortable with the narratives that have been presented to us. But stubbornness, pride, and human reasoning keep us from embracing a Kingdom mindset. We see this in Mark 12: 13-17. In this passage, the Herodians and Pharisees attempt to lure Jesus into their net. After they questioned Jesus about the civil practice of taxation, He ups the ante. *And He said to them, "Whose image and inscription is this?" They said to Him, "Caesar's." And Jesus answered and said to them. Render to Caesar the things that are Caesar's and to God the things that are God's." And they marveled at Him.* They were stumped. If God is Creator, in whose image they were created, then based on their reasoning, they must pay tribute to God. Jesus knew they were being hypocritical and showed them the state of their hearts. When we embrace a Kingdom mindset, human reasoning becomes shallow.

Jesus' humble posture puzzled onlookers, who expected someone of apparent regal position to be the Messiah. They had a preconceived idea of what the Messiah should be, and he dismantled it in his manner, his life, and his words. Jesus' perspective is radical and hard for us to digest sometimes. How would you react if Jesus told you that he wants you to interact with mean, domineering people, but be gentle and wise? *Beware of everyone, for some of these people will file police reports on you and punish you in front of their congregations. You will be taken against your will to civil leaders because you stand for me, to reflect me to them and all unbelievers.*[9] (Tina's paraphrase).

If we are honest with ourselves, we don't like some of his teachings. If our spouse committed adultery, would we say, "Rise, no one condemns you, go and sin no more"? While his statement reflects both a legal and spiritual act of forgiveness and the lifting off of shame, as human beings, we find ourselves preferring separation, divorce, name-calling, and long seasons of counseling. Not to say that divorce or counseling in this situation is unbiblical, but Jesus' actions towards the sinner, even before the cross, defies our sense of personal justice.

When we read the gospels slowly, we see how often Jesus shows the Jews the hypocrisy of their mindsets,

---

[9] Matthew 10:17-19 But beware of men, for they will hand you over to *the* courts and scourge you in their synagogues; [18] and you will even be brought before governors and kings for My sake, as a testimony to them and to the Gentiles. [19] But when they hand you over, do not worry about how or what you are to say; for it will be given you in that hour what you are to say.

especially in the way they think of the Samaritans. The lesson of the Samaritan is that no matter how offended, stigmatized, and discriminated against, the offended—the victim has the ability to help the oppressor with genuine love and compassion. If you identify yourself as an oppressed person, a victim, or someone who has faced injustice, are you willing to show compassion to the one (or group) who oppressed you?

Purposely Born into Oppression
What are we to think about a God who chooses an ethnic group that would be murdered by the millions and despised by most nations from which to reveal His grace and Truth? Jesus, the incarnate Christ, took on Middle Eastern skin tones and features; his ancestors were comprised of an adulterer-murderer and a prostitute. The testimony of Jesus is that no matter the degree of oppression, His version of justice allows for the wronged to overcome. The victim triumphs over evil by operating in a manner opposite of the oppressor.

Questions:
- As you study the Gospels, what disposition is required for the oppressed to love their enemies?

- To what extent do you see Christ's response to sin, self-righteousness, and injustice reflected in how you live your life?

- "The Church needs to deal with racial injustice." If this is your view, on what basis do you make this statement? Is a Sunday morning sermon discussing the sin of prejudice enough?

- How do you determine if a Christian brother or sister's words or actions are complicit with skin-tone bias (racial prejudice)? (This question can expand to skin-tone bias within the black community, Latino community, or elitism within the white community, especially when it comes to economics) Can you find Biblical support for the reasoning that you use?

2

Christ's Emotional Response to Injustice

"Not all cops are racist."
"Defund the police."
"Systemic racism isn't real."
"Law and order."

At least one of these phrases makes you angry. Me too. No matter what angle we take on racial injustice or the solutions, our aggravation with opposing views can seem justified when we think their view is unbiblical.

A few months ago, when the news concerning the Amhaud Arbery shooting first began sweeping across the news cycle, I (Chris) found myself wrestling with deep anger for several days. As I saw many others doing, I often felt led to post my thoughts on social media, to explain how what was going on was affecting me, to helpfully provide another perspective that people would find beneficial amidst the conflicting opinions of secular media. And yet, every time I moved to write something, I could never find peace. Finally, when it became too much to bear, I poured out all my thoughts into my journal, all the anger, all the concern, all the turmoil. And then, I listened. I asked the Lord to help me see what he saw, and to help me to think as he did. And he did.

A couple of weeks later, still quarantined at home due to the Covid-19 pandemic, George Floyd was murdered. In the rush of reactions and counterreactions, I began to feel that same frustration and anger I had felt a few weeks prior. And that same compulsion to say something and that same check in my spirit not to. Again, it seemed the only outlet I had permission to express myself was to my family and God. And so, I did. After every conversation with various family members, I tried to leave space to listen, to see what God would say to me. And, perhaps surprisingly to some of you, he always did.

I've had several moments like that since then, and only a couple of times have I felt released to speak on it or post on social media. But over the past several months, I have noticed a shift, that the check and pause before saying something is no longer a surprise; I anticipate it. And I realize that over the last few months, the Lord has been teaching me how to discern when He is prompting me to say something versus when my emotions are behind the urge to say something. Through this process, I've realized that my heart for justice is not always aligned with his. What bothers me is often not what bothers him and what I initially feel called to say is not often what I hear him saying. So, I am confronted with this question. *Is my pursuit of justice for him or me? Is my subconscious motivation to satisfy the impulses of my soul? Or to honor Him and see His Kingdom and His manifest on earth?* If the latter, then I've realized that the only way forward is to live out a Spirit-led life.

I've noticed that some people struggle with how to relate to their emotions. Years ago, one of my students broke down in tears, overcome with anger, frustration, and disappointment when certain goals were not met. Then, referring to their breakdown, they said, "I hate my body for this weakness!" They feared the strength and unpredictable expression of their emotions, and therefore despised them. They had always prided themselves on a purely logical approach to life.

This response grieved my soul. Our emotions, while never meant to run our lives, are gifts from God. We are made in the image of an emotional God. And unfortunately, I find it quite common within the church that while we know what to do with our emotions when we play sports, we don't always know how to bring our emotions into our relationship with God, into our worship, our prayer lives, our serving, or our response to injustice.

A Heart to Heart with The Pain Of The Broken

Strong expressions of emotions overwhelm me. It is easy to allow judgment to enter my heart when I observe people who lead with their emotions, people that respond to situations in ways that I think are clearly irrational. The truth of the matter is that my judgment is not by the Spirit. My aversion does not come from a place of wholeness. I used to be similar to my logic-minded student—cool, calm, and collected. In reality, I was simply repressing my emotions; and even *that,* I wasn't doing very well. I had been simply rationalizing the messages that my emotions were feeding me. I was reasoning from an emotional place; my thought process was carried away by the current of unnamed and unaddressed emotions in my soul.

Contrary to what we may have been told, there are not two groups of people in the world: logical and emotional. We are all emotional, and we all must learn to embrace our emotions as a gift, a gift that needs to be purified and submitted to Christ, but a gift, nonetheless.

Romans 8 tells us that we are all being conformed to the image of Christ. Ephesians tells us to be imitators of God. And both these epistles also tell us that the renewal of our minds births this transformation. We must think differently. **If we truly want to display Christ's response to injustice, we cannot just think of the way he thinks about injustice, *we must also feel the way he feels.*** And for many of us, that means thinking differently about emotion.

One cannot read the Old Testament without concluding that God experiences a full range of emotions. Particularly through the writings of the prophets, we see anger, frustration, grief, compassion, joy, and delight, all ultimately expressions of his great love for us. When the Israelites were suffering under unjust rulers, when the shepherds neglect their responsibility for the flock, we consistently observe God reacting emotionally to this injustice. Out of deep compassion for those being hurt and oppressed, he executes judgment on the oppressor and promises deliverance and freedom for the oppressed.

We see this echoed throughout the gospels. Many of Jesus' miracles involve him being moved with compassion for the sick, the lame, the demon oppressed. The wholeness of who he is committed to seeking justice for the one who suffers. Does he do it based only on emotion? Devoid of intellect? No. Jesus is led only by the Holy Spirit and not the emotions of others. Yet, he understands the emotional response of others. For instance, he did not rebuke Mary for crying when Lazarus, her brother, was dead. His emotions are engaged, and they are whole and submitted to God.

Our social media newsfeeds display both apathy, dismay, and overwhelming grief. The Bible never chastises the oppressed who cry out for loudly crying out. A lament is a healthy way to process grief. The point is not that those who cry every day need to cry less, and those who rarely cry ought to be in constant tears. My point is that there are things worth crying about in this world and our lives. Emotions allow us to express our humanity and reflect God's love. We must review our emotional responses or lack thereof by submitting them to the Spirit of God, as revealed in the Bible. Being yielded to Him and aware of our brokenness will help us to express our emotions in a healthy way when confronted with the reality of injustice.

If we truly want to respond to injustice as Christ would, we cannot enter a conversation with the mind of God while leaving his heart at home. We need the wisdom of God to know what to do, but the heart of God to know how to do it, aiming to imitate Christ in all things.

Questions:

• What role do your emotions play in your response to injustice?

• As you study Jesus' responses to injustice, would he view your emotional response to injustice (or lack thereof) as an obstacle to be overcome? Why or why not?

• Do you generally ignore and suppress your emotions? Do you quickly vent them to others before lamenting with the Lord? If so, why do you think this is?

• How can you begin to treat your emotions as welcome gifts that are part of who you are as an imager of God?

Be Angry and Sin Not[10]

Any display of God's emotions is rational, good, and healthy. As we look into Scripture, this truth confounds us, comforts us, and sometimes *offends* us.

---

[10] Ephesians 4:26-32 But don't let the passion of your emotions lead you to sin! Don't let anger control you or be fuel for revenge, not for even a day. Don't give the slanderous accuser, the devil, an opportunity to manipulate you! If anyone of you has stolen from someone else, never do it again. Instead, be industrious, earning an honest living, and then you'll have enough to bless those in need. (TPT)

We are encouraged when Jesus weeps at the burial tomb of his friend, even though he knows he is going to resurrect him. We are glad that his compassion welcomes children and protects his mother in her old age by entrusting John as her steward. On the other hand, we scratch our heads when he eats a meal with immoral people and overturns the tables in the temple. The effort that he exerted, which probably broke some of the merchandise from which the sellers based their livelihood, tells us that his zeal for worship outweighed his concern for their provision. More bewildering are the times when in his zeal for righteousness, God instructs the Israelites to destroy tribes that worshipped differently. How does this emotional response instruct us? God's anger is just and appropriate and never evil. Paul warns us that *we* have the propensity to sin when we are angry, especially if we are quick to speak and slow to hear. We must go before God and acknowledge our tendency to be triggered and react before asking him, "How should I respond?" Becoming emotionally healthy requires us to go to our prayer closets and our Bibles to find out what God would have us say and what God would have us do.

As we find out how God would have us practically respond to injustice, we must keep in mind that honest dialogue, legislation, and protest can be emotionally satisfying, but they cannot renew the minds of those who do evil. As long as hearts stay unaligned with God's intent, injustice will remain.

Questions

- As Christians, if God views humanity as two camps: (kingdom of his Son and kingdom of darkness), yet desires to bring the wicked to repentance, (and we were once the wicked), then as proclaimers of the gospel, how should we respond to those whose sins lead to injustice?

- For believers who serve in levels of civil government, law enforcement, or the judicial sphere, how can they reflect Jesus' Kingdom perspective?

- How do we mirror Jesus so that the wicked have an opportunity to be delivered from their sin, yet allow them to experience the consequences of their wickedness?

Executing Justice While Embracing Emotion

The oppressed know why they are in pain, but accurately pointing out a problem does not mean they know the correct solution. People don't make wise decisions when in pain, and for believers, our own pain often makes it difficult to hear and be led by the Spirit. When I am angry, I do not see the situation clearly—I'm filtering it through my pain. Here is another situation that I (Chris) had while teaching.

It was April Fool's Day of 2017. I'd heard some vague rumors that some of my 10th graders were going to pull a prank, but I thought they'd be smart enough not to. (This was foolish on my part, but I was new at teaching). I walked into class, and they had pushed some of the chairs and tables out through the window and put others behind the divider in the classroom. They thought I'd appreciate their cleverness. All of us were disappointed that day. I was MAD. It wasn't red hot rage, but the ice-cold, *I am going to very slowly and painfully show you how wrong you are to do this* kind of mad. And boy did my 'righteous' anger blow up in my face.

I learned a hard but useful lesson that day. In the aftermath of the mess, I asked myself: What had been my goal in my manner? What should it have been? Why did I want to lecture them the way I did? The answer was my pride and self-righteousness. I was more committed to making a big deal of why what they did was an inconvenience and negatively affected me, than displaying mercy and compassion as I communicated how bad decisions hurt relationships. My dawning later that night could only have come from God because only God knows how to balance justice and mercy.

In the moments when we get hurt or offended, we are going to fall back on the habits of "the old man[11]." I realized after that incident that I hadn't formed a new default that I could fall back on so that I could yield to the Holy Spirit in times of crisis. Despite being offended, I should have paused, maybe even stepped into the hall, and prayed. I wish I had admitted my anger but released it to God; dropped my mission to be able to fulfill his.

Executing appropriate measures of justice doesn't happen by accident. Fully embracing the ways of God is a process—it takes time to change how we think. Also, Scripture tells us that the transformation God brings to

---

[11] Colossians 3:9 Don't lie to each other, for you have stripped off your old sinful nature and all its wicked deeds.

our lives, while birthed in our hearts, is ultimately exposed in our thinking, and then visible through our words and actions.

I love the way Paul describes the Christian life.[12] He says that we hold such power in our jars of clay.[13] We are not capable of solving all the problems of this world. But we don't have to be. Our ability to access and yield to God isn't hindered if we don't have it all together or if we're mad, stressed, condemned, tired, or whatever else we might think would disqualify us. Our dependence is our glory, the place where Christ's power is made perfect in our weakness.

I share these stories to make this final point. We ought not to be overwhelmed by the problems of our age. We were made to be dependent on God, to live shoulder to shoulder, and face to face with the Overcomer. Humankind was never meant to eat from the tree of the knowledge of good and evil. God never wanted us to know everything. Why? Because *he* was there walking with us in the garden to reveal to us whatever we might want and need to know. We had access to him, we didn't need what the tree offered. Thankfully Jesus died, and the curtain was torn so that intimacy might be restored to us once again. God has every solution we need and wants to reveal to us. We need to stop thinking that he expects us to know anything without asking him. He is hoping that we'll see our dependence as a reason to rejoice because it means we get to solve the problems of the world *with* him. We can learn from him as he guides us into all truth, reveals

---

[12] 2 Corinthians 3 (whole chapter)
[13] 2 Corinthians 4:7 But we have this treasure in jars of clay, to show that the surpassing power belongs to God and not to us. (ESV)

his solutions, and reveals more of his goodness and character to our hearts. If we can choose to see life this way, the desperate situations and circumstances that arise can cause us to have great joy. Why? Because they are invitations to walk more closely to the heart of God, to live from his love towards us, so we might be led by his Spirit, and fulfill and accomplish his works of justice on the earth.

3

Where does Oppression Begin?

What comes first, the chicken or the egg? Or, if I (Chris) can amend this saying for our purposes, what comes first, the system of oppression or the person with a heart susceptible to the abuse of power? The purpose of this section is to establish the latter and to argue that any attempt to undo systemic injustice that ignores freeing individuals from spiritual bondage and oppression will be insufficient and unsustainable. A brief look at some scriptural case studies will paint a clear picture for us.

Let's start in Genesis.

Genesis 3 contains the first tragedy in human history. The chapter goes on to describe how the sin of humanity spirals into systemic injustice. After God comes down and prompts Adam and Eve to reveal the sin they've committed, he declares that a curse will now affect humanity and the world. While humans will struggle with the ground (work) and experience toil and futility instead of abundant harvests (provision), God states that the first place injustice will express itself is in the marriage relationship. Part of the curse humanity incurred is that a wife's desire will be for her husband, and he will lord over her.[14] Rather than operating as co-regents over creation, couples will engage in a continual power struggle in a posture of loving self-sacrifice from husband to wife and loving submission from wife to husband. Mutual respect, loving self-sacrifice, and loving submission are stripped from the original equation. Now under the curse of sin, marriage will be a relationship of conflict, stress, and competition. But marriage will not be the only relationship where conflict, stress, and competition will occur.

Before Genesis 3, Adam and Eve had been walking intimately with God for an unknown amount of time. Their ways of operating were only from wholeness and love. There were no corrupt human systems in existence. Although evil was a reality within the unseen spiritual realm, the first couple knew only good. But sin corrupts God's original intent, and in Genesis 4, we witness the first murder recorded in Scripture. Then Genesis 6 gives us a shocking analysis of the state of humanity.

The Lord saw how great the wickedness of the human race had become on the earth, and that every inclination of the thoughts of the human heart was only evil all the time. The Lord regretted that he had made human beings on the

---

[14] Genesis 3:16 To the woman he said, I will surely multiply your pain in childbearing; in pain you shall bring forth children. Your desire shall be contrary to your husband, but he shall rule over you.

earth, and his heart was deeply troubled. So the Lord said, "I will wipe from the face of the earth the human race I have created—and with them the animals, the birds and the creatures that move along the ground—for I regret that I have made them." But Noah found favor in the eyes of the Lord. Genesis 6:5-8, NIV

What a scathing rebuke of the human condition! Surely at this point, a thousand years after the Fall, mechanisms of systemic inequality and oppression had been established. How could they not? Yet, Scripture does not highlight *that* as the problem. No, the wickedness of humanity is tracked directly to the corruption of the human heart. To the extent that the human heart is a slave to sin, evil and oppression of all kinds will be expressed in society.

Do Systems Corrupt People, Or Do People Corrupt Systems?

Corruption of the heart is revealed to us again after the divine reset—the Flood. God restarts humanity from the seed of one man, Noah, the only person found righteous before the Flood. But we very quickly learn that Noah's righteousness is not a heart immune from sin; rather, a righteousness that comes from obedience and trust in God. Noah still wrestles with internal bondage to sin.

If Noah is a godly man, (Scripture tells us he and his family are the only human beings that were allowed to live), how could systems of oppression form if not from the hearts of his descendants? By Genesis 11 and 12, most of humanity has again fallen away from God, despising his commands to be fruitful and fill the earth. Instead of building according to his dominion mandate, they build a symbol of human pride. The people came together; built a tower (Babel) to reach the heavens so they could make a name for themselves. For themselves. This is key. Their heart disposition would negate the significance of being made in the image of God. As a consequence, God must intervene once again, not with a flood, but by confusing the languages of humankind.

This pattern continues throughout the Old Testament. Even after witnessing the favor of the Lord during their escape through the Red Sea, the Israelites build a golden calf to worship. This event happens while Moses is receiving the Law from God on Mount Sinai. After the unbelieving Israelites die in the wilderness for their sin and after their descendants have possessed the promised land, another falling away occurs. The book of Judges explains that after Joshua and his contemporaries had died, the nation of Israel was enticed by the pagan people groups that they had not driven from the land.

We even see this tendency toward heart corruption with King David, a man after God's own heart. David was still in bondage to sin and spiritual oppression. While this is most notably revealed in his affair with Bathsheba and the murder of her husband, Uriah, we see this bondage through his polygamy. He deviated from the pattern God established in Genesis of one man and one woman for life. David is also not a great father. Several of his sons attempt to overthrow his throne at one point or another. His son, Solomon, is a man filled with great wisdom from God, but that wisdom is a grace gift, extended due to God's lavish favor and generosity, not some inner purity on Solomon's part. Solomon falls away in his later years due to marrying pagan women and allowing the worship of their idols to be established in his Kingdom. The kings after Solomon are even worse. The canon of Scripture reveals that kings who follow the way of the Lord are few and far between; the result is systemic oppression and judgment upon the people of Israel.

What Does This Mean for Us Today?

The return to a just kingdom is always preceded by repentance—an acknowledgment of the causal/foundational sin that is rebellion against God and his ways. This pattern is found throughout the Old Testament. All systemic corruption proceeded from a fallen state that would find no remedy until the cross.

Jesus affirms the necessity of repentance. In Luke 4, after coming out of the wilderness full of the power of the Spirit, Jesus goes to the synagogue and reads from Isaiah 61.

> *The Spirit of the Lord is on me because he has anointed me to proclaim good news to the poor. He has sent me to proclaim freedom for the prisoners and recovery of sight for the blind, to set the oppressed free, to proclaim the year of the Lord's favor.[15]*

---

[15] Luke 4:18-19 NIV

After this declaration, Jesus tells people to repent because the Kingdom of Heaven is at hand. He preaches the good news of the Kingdom. Everywhere he goes, he heals the sick, casts out demons, heals the lame, provides sight to the blind, and even raises the dead. And he does all of this among God's chosen people who are currently under the power and authority of the Roman empire.

The Gospels tell us that systemic oppression and injustice is going on during the time of Jesus. Many verses reference corrupt military officers abusing their authority, corrupt tax collectors who take more than required, and corrupt religious officials who care about prestige more than people. Yet, we don't see Jesus attacking the systems they represent; we see him going straight to the heart of the matter (pun intended). He speaks directly about their spiritual bondage and heart corruption and then calls individuals to live holy lives. Some repent, like Zacchaeus, Matthew the disciple, Jairus, and the Roman centurion. Jesus displays the lavish love and goodness of God by dispensing their requests, healing for a servant, and a daughter. Throughout the gospels, Jesus makes advance withdraws on the redemption he will accomplish through his death on the cross and even forgives sin. He calls people to recognize the internal poverty of their lives and teaches that despite the circumstances around them, freedom and peace are available if they would return to God.

Furthermore, our Lord reveals that spiritual forces are seeking to perpetuate the brokenness and oppression among us (more on that in a later chapter). Just like in the Garden, the devil seeks to perpetuate his agenda:

disconnecting us from God first, each other second, and then using us as instruments of division to further brokenness in the earth. To undermine the tactics of these forces, Jesus calls us to walk in forgiveness and relational wholeness with each other.

Jesus knows that his earthly Kingdom will be manifested to the extent that his rule is established in the hearts of men. Where sin sits on the throne of a human heart, goodness, even good intentions, will be hindered and perverted. But where repentance occurs, and the work of the Christ applied to the lives of broken men and women, life-giving relationships can happen.

Here's the rub when it comes to injustice. Many of us are fighting for a change that cannot happen without repentance through salvation. Morality cannot be legislated. We cannot protect people from injustice. It is going to happen.

As Christ sits on the throne of our hearts and grows the seed of His Word into life-supplying fruit, corrupt systems are dismantled brick by brick. It is the Lord's desire for us to promote and sustain a society where justice reigns. But the heart is the starting point.

Questions:
- To what extent can believers *expect* non-Christian leaders to uphold God's stance on punishing evildoers? (1 Peter 2:14)

- According to biblical precedent, what can believers do to guarantee that civil authorities punish the people, organizations, and corporations that either 1) pass unjust laws, 2) give unjust consequences, or 3)treat people unjustly?

- Since civil law cannot stop corruption, which stems from the heart, what expectation does God want us to have for how effective civil authority can be when addressing injustice?

- How are we to apply Proverbs 21:1 to civil authorities in light of the fact that God never causes anyone to sin? *"The king's heart is like channels of water in the hand of the Lord; He turns it wherever He wishes."* (NASB)

4

Tale of Two Kingdoms

Throughout the Bible, God separates humankind into two groups. In the New Testament, we find those who receive Him and become part of the "kingdom of His beloved Son" and those who remain in the "domain of darkness" (Col 1:13) unless they choose to receive salvation. These groups are also referred to as the circumcised and uncircumcised, or Israel and the Gentiles. Ephesians 2 tells us that every human being is born belonging to the latter kingdom. When we read this chapter of Ephesians, we see words like "alienated" and "darkened." Paul uses these words to inform us about our nature, our orientation to God's standard, and the disposition of our minds before we are born again[16].

When I think about the events of the last couple of months-the brutal death of an arrested black man, the subsequent protests, the peaceful marches, as well as the

---

[16] John 3:3 Jesus answered and said to him, "Most assuredly, I say to you, unless one is born again, he cannot see the kingdom of God." (NKJV)

despicable looting, I divide the participants into the same two groups that God does. Why? Because those who are no longer darkened in their minds now have the ability to address these events with the mind of the Spirit. The others do not.

Because of this, my assessment of our present divisive climate is not based on ethnicity or to be specific: skin tone and the history that comes with it. Regularly, I push aside the narrative that white people are racists or *privileged*, and people of color are victims. That is a human view, not a Biblical lens. I must consider the Bible's two groups: the spiritual haves and have nots (those who have salvation and those that don't) and discern *whose ideas*—sinner or redeemed—steer the conversations about injustice.

What is our appropriate goal for eradicating injustice? As believers, our dilemma is that we cannot expect sinners to treat each person with kindness, dignity, and honor for any sustained amount of time. Maybe you've heard the phrase, "Sinners sin." This phrase merely reminds the "haves" that people who do not have peace with Christ cannot be expected to have the capacity to be Christlike. Therefore, our current affairs are more than a problem of white vs. non-white and systemic racism, although those symptoms *must* be dealt with. The problem or battle is with the mind—reasonings and views that are not aligned with God. We must target the ideas that form people's opinions of others. Are these ideas in agreement with God's design and intent for humankind? Or are they *-isms* based on doctrines of devils? Many believers are demanding a change in people's discriminatory actions and ensuing behaviors. But this demand is both unreasonable and unrealistic if the offender is not even saved.

The Biblical explanation of a sin-stained heart and unrenewed mind is a hard pill to swallow. It means that I (Tina) cannot blame my high school administrator for blocking my attempts to begin a Minority Student Union. At the time, I was confused and angry. *What can 32 black kids out of 2000 students possibly do that threatens him?* My confusion and anger are gone now because I see view him through a biblical lens. Likewise, I do not blame the cashier at a local store that refused to take my order. I stood at the counter thinking. *Is what is going on what I think is going on?* After a moment, my white friend asserted herself, and the cashier "woke up" and asked me for my order. The truth is, some people do not have the capacity to honor me and respect me. I cannot expect them to do so for one of two reasons: 1) They have not exchanged their sin-laden lives for the righteousness of Christ or 2) They have spiritual or iniquitous mental strongholds that keep them blinded and carnally-minded.[17]

Prejudice in the Church

Immaturity, lack of discipleship, and spiritual blindness are why racism still occurs in the Church. Many of our fellow believers are babies in their spiritual *and* emotional maturity[18]. Either they have not been discipled

---

[17] Romans 8:5 Those who are motivated by the flesh only pursue what benefits themselves. But those who live by the impulses of the Holy Spirit are motivated to pursue spiritual realities. (TPT)

[18] Hebrews 5:3 For everyone who partakes *only* of milk *is* un-skilled in the word of righteousness, for he is a babe. (NKJV)

well, or the thief has been able to blind them to the error of their ways and thinking.

Some of the dirty laundry in the Church reveals that some of us, past and present, have not treated others with kindness, dignity, and honor. Although I (Tina) will focus on race discrimination, this is not the only issue where our sin of mistreatment occurs. The mistreatment of other people is historic and has occurred on every continent and in every generation since Christ. It causes us to question the validity of the offender's salvation. *How could any of the slave-owning Founding Fathers have really been Christians? How could a true Christian vote for President Trump?* I understand why these questions come about. But here is a question I have had: *If salvation regenerates a person's essence, freeing them from the bondage of sin and the consequence of eternal separation from God, then how could a redeemed man or woman ever treat someone based on the color of their skin or any other external factor?*

To put it simply, some Christians—even leaders have not rid their minds of ungodly, darkened, fleshly viewpoints during their faith journey. Despite this reality, as the body of Christ, and despite our imperfections, we can be used as instruments of reconciliation. But our *primary* focus cannot be in the reconciling of ethnicities, rather a reconciling of God's enemies to Himself. As stated repeatedly in the previous chapters, vertical alignment from the human heart to God's authority is required for person-to-person reconciliation to be possible. So racial reconciliation cannot be a *universal goal* when there are two groups of citizens of two opposing kingdoms, and where one kingdom—the kingdom of Jesus—contains a disappointing number of unrenewed minds.

> When I was a child, I used to speak like a child, think like a child, reason like a child; when I became a man, I did away with childish things. [19]

> And do not be conformed to this world, but be transformed by the renewing of your mind, so that you may prove what the will of God is, that which is good and acceptable and perfect. [20]

Did Jesus Discriminate?

Some people may say that Jesus was never around people of different skin colors or ethnicities because he lived among Jews and Romans. But in order to have been tempted on all counts-even the temptation to treat someone poorly, he had to have come in contact with them. Jesus saw the differences, but the differences didn't deter him from showing kindness, dignity, and honor.

I remember when I first read Matthew 15:26-27. *And He answered and said, "It is not good to take the children's bread and throw it to the dogs. But she said, "Yes, Lord; but even the dogs feed on the crumbs which fall from their masters' table."*

I was horrified! He called this woman a dog because she was not a Jew! However, Jesus was making a statement that there is a divine separation of people

---

[19] 1 Corinthians 13: 11 NASB

[20] Romans 12:2 NASB

according to the kingdoms that I mentioned above. In short, as a Canaanite, the woman represents those born outside of God's covenant/promise. The Jewish people were descendants of Jacob, the bearer of the promise.

When talking to the woman, Jesus was not condemning her for being born a sinner. I think he was finding out whether she knew her position outside of the promise and whether she understood what he came to offer and why. His bread—his life was sent first to the children of Israel. Her use of his reference to dogs reveals that she recognizes her position and that he is the one with the highest position and authority. However, she pleads that those outside of the covenant would be nourished by that which he has to offer.

Jesus came to differentiate people based on whether they were in covenant with Him, the son of God. The words discriminate and discrimination involve **the ability and authority to make distinctions and to discern differences**. This discrimination—differentiation is godly and meant to lead people into the path of righteousness.

The kingdom of "God's dear Son" is comprised of people whose confession of faith is centers of the person and resurrection of Jesus Christ. The circumcision of the male foreskin in the Old Testament was a foreshadowing of the circumcision of the heart that salvation brings. In God's eyes, the circumcised are those who obtain righteousness through faith, not by works. All others are uncircumcised and belong to the kingdom of darkness.

Why did Jesus heal the Canaanite woman? I believe it was because she came in faith in who he was. As my son Chris said earlier, he made an early withdrawal from the power of the cross. He could do this because, legally, he was already the Lamb slain before the foundation of the world.

Whether the truth of covenant distinction among human beings makes us uncomfortable or not, we live in a world where there are kind people around us who are outside of the covenant. The Bible explains to us how God views their nature and their mindset. So as Jesus followers, like it or not, we must view unbelievers the same way. We cannot listen to the words of others, the narratives, media outlets, candidates, and *not* discriminate. It is our duty to discern human solutions from God's solutions.

The reason I'm delving into this is that when I read non-mainstream news articles or clips, I see people of *every* skin tone upset because of the injustice that comes with treating a person based on their skin tone. This is good. But I also see:

- People of every skin tone violently lashing out, promoting or inciting anarchy.
- People of every skin tone defensive and angry.
- People of every skin tone vying for solutions through political means.
- People of every skin color who call themselves Christians, call people names and speak unkindly.

And never let ugly or hateful words come from your mouth, but instead, let your words become beautiful gifts that encourage others; do this by speaking words of grace to help them.[21]

We cannot be the trouble-shooters and solution-givers if we get caught up in the fray and indiscriminately link arms with those who are outside of the covenant. Am I saying that we cannot work together and engage with unbelievers to limit injustice? No. I am reminding us that Scripture instructs us to "walk not in the counsel of the wicked". When we come to the table, we need to have already sought the Lord's counsel in our prayer closets and through Bible study, so that we can offer His wisdom, not our filtered reasoning.

What started as needed public outcry for the murder of black males grew into a legitimate focus on police protocol, but now has revealed the deficit of conversation about the only lasting way to healing

Questions:

- As we look through the lens of kingdom-citizenship (unsaved vs born again), what Bible scriptures can you find that apply to those who carry the sword and wield it unjustly? (carry the sword represents those in authority, those tasked to punish crime).

- Read Matthew 15:26. If you heard a leader (e.g., pastor, political leader, movement leader) call someone a "dog", how would you respond? Why was this not prejudiced or discriminatory for Jesus to call the woman a "dog"? (Strong's G2965 – a puppy, dog)

---

[21] Eph 4: 29 TPT

- In regard to "white privilege" or the privilege of the majority ethnic group/skin color in a nation, what can those with "majority privilege" do to make sure that all people have equal opportunities? Give your biblical basis. In our nation, this applies to those of European heritage, however, in Asia, this would apply to Asians.

- Using the above question, if the majority population of a nation was believers, what could they do to make sure non-believers have equal opportunities? How does this apply to the sense of injustice that some people incur regarding who they marry?

- Is the current mission of the social justice movement to pursue equal opportunity supported in Scripture? What passages would you use to support that and why?

5

Justice God's Way

Let's look at the reasons why some Jews were offended and rejected Jesus. Many of them looked for a political leader to deliver them from the tyranny of Rome. For others, their familiarity with Him as "one of their own" was a stumbling block. And for the religious leaders, his teachings pointed out their faults and spoke against what they believed. Their version of justice was an eye for an eye (Matthew 5:38). His was simply, "Do not retaliate." In order words, He was pointing out that their religious version of justice was ungodly.

In a recent sermon, our pastor pointed out that an eye for an eye would have left both parties blind. What good does this penalty for injustice do for society? It is neither restorative nor productive. As the passage continues, we read Jesus' recommendation to a Jewish person when a Roman soldier commands them to carry his supplies to exhibit their domination. Jesus advises, "Whoever forces you to go one mile, go with him two."

Jesus' advice elevates the victim above the oppressor by telling the victim to go another mile, meaning *take the upper hand in the situation and make the oppressor face his unjust manner*. Jesus' way of dealing with injustice focuses on getting the oppressor to see their heart.

Jesus, The Rock of Offense

"Behold, I lay in Zion a chief cornerstone, elect, precious, and he who believes on Him will by no means be put to shame. Therefore, to you who believe, He is precious; but to those who are disobedient, "The stone which the builders rejected Has become the chief cornerstone, and "A stone of stumbling And a rock of offense." They stumble, being disobedient to the word, to which they also were appointed (1 Peter 2:6-8).

Why does the Bible teach that Jesus is offensive? Because some will not like His teachings. Scripture goes on to say that those who refuse him and are offended by him will be put to shame.

Jesus defines what justice is supposed to be for all of us. This is troubling because some believers propose that some form of retaliation is justified and even necessary to subdue oppression. But what does retaliation mean? Retaliation means giving someone what they deserve. We must make sure that God is the definer of *what they deserve*. Am I suggesting that we let people off the hook for their actions? No, but we must assess 1) how God views their actions and 2) the why behind the consequences we want for them to have. We need to inspect our motives. We also need to compare what we consider to be unjust with what God considers to be unjust.

Because we want to center on our motivations before discussing civil consequences, it is important to find out whether we are asking more of others than we ask of ourselves. In other words, is our fight for justice somewhat hypocritical?

For example:

- Have you "served time," so to speak, for all the sins you've committed?
- Could a godly judge ever model God, the Judge, by releasing a person from a sentence based on their verbal repentance? If you believe that would not be satisfying for you, do you know why?
- Have you apologized to everyone you've ever hurt, intentionally or unintentionally? Or paid for their time and suffering?
- Have you made sure their need for justice (the person you sinned against) was met for *every* transgression you committed?

None of us have done this. Therefore, you and I, as people that have offended and hurt others, walk free and clear. We have not paid the price for our injustice and oppression. We have apologized (hopefully), and then expected the ones we hurt to do what Jesus says, stop throwing stones and forgive 77 times 7!

The Price of Forgiveness

You and I were not alive when Christ died for the cross, and yet all our sins, past, present, and future, were atoned for 2000 years ago. If that's true for us, is that not also true for everyone? Although their sins have not been appropriated by faith through salvation, their sins *have* been paid for. This reality helps us hone in on our motives and our self-righteousness.

Since Christ has paid for our sins, we are now seen as guiltless before God; this is atonement and justification. Christ's death on the cross atones (pays for) our sin so that we are justified—able to walk shameless and clean before Him.

Can you see what this means for our pursuit of justice? All injustice has been paid for already! Justice has been executed! Not on the person who committed the act of injustice, but on Jesus. Every injustice, whether it be racism, assault, abuse of power, discrimination, and anything else that can occur in this fallen world, was paid for on the cross. In God's eyes, judgment has been served, so now he can pursue a *restorative* course that flows from his heart. Reconciliation with the evildoers. Healing of relationships. The cross not only makes way for forgiveness and mercy, but it also allows us to come into the presence of the One who can heal us from injustice.

Although God is a place of safety, he is also a stumbling block, a trap, and a snare.[22] What does a trap do? It captures, binds, and denies freedom. In this verse, God is not only addressing the house of Israel, but also the

---

[22] Isaiah 8:14 He will be as a sanctuary, But a stone of stumbling and a rock of offense To both the houses of Israel, As a trap and a snare to the inhabitants of Jerusalem.

inhabitants of Jerusalem. When it comes to deciding what is unjust, we are not free to decide on our own. We are bound to Him, bondservants of our Lord and Savior. Truth—God's truth will be a snare when we accept a course toward justice that is not his.

The Cross Vs. Civil Consequences

How does the cross change what we pursue when faced with civil injustice and oppression? Repeated and continual exposure to blatant murder and a faulty judicial system can wear on us emotionally. Cynicism, prayerlessness, and fear-based responses show how hopeless many of us feel and how conditioned we have become to expect the worst from both people and systems. It has become easy for our pursuit of justice to be *less* about a desire for restorative consequences, but rather out of a need to express our emotional distress *and* see someone else suffer. We are often not actually after God's justice; we just want to get even. We're after punishment, not repentance that leads to reconciliation and relational wholeness.

There is a place for civil consequences, but first, let's address what the Bible says about vengeance, punishment, and retribution.

Vengeance Is Mine. I Will Repay!

But it is taking too long, Lord! is the thought of many people of color, women, and even many Christians. Let's look at some Bible accounts to see how God's repayment can look.

While retribution, a prison sentence, restitution, capital punishment, and legislation have biblical precedents, we need to understand what they cannot do. They won't heal the victim of the trauma of the experience. They cannot return a victim's emotional security or wellbeing. God can and wants to provide for that deep healing, the restoration of spirit, soul, and body. He can do that regardless of whether or not the oppressor ever comes under earthly justice.

In the same way that we can forgive without having received an apology, we can be healed and recover without civil consequences being met. This is a hard fact, especially for Christians of color or any victim of any injustice. Our wounds can be healed. The process of executing imperfect earthly justice no longer has to stand between us and living a life of freedom and healing in Christ. So, when it comes to the justice system, we do not have to be bound emotionally to its imperfections. God can make us whole and heal us from victimization at any time if we are willing to go to him and receive. Our motivation for justice is no longer about satisfying our need for the offender to be punished. It is about seeing the offended, and the offender offered a restorative path to wholeness.

Genesis 4:10 gives us a critical foundation for understanding God's heart for all of humankind. Cain and Abel were the first children of Adam and Eve that we read about. Theirs was the first generation born under bondage to sin. Interestingly enough, before Cain murders his brother, God speaks to him: "Why are you angry? And why has your countenance fallen? If you do well, will not your countenance be lifted up? And if you do not do well, sin is crouching at the door; and its desire is for you, but you must master it." The next verse reveals that Cain did not do what God said he had the power to do: master sin.

Sin had not been atoned, although God had already initiated a system of justice for taking a life. In the previous chapter, after Adam and Eve had taken their own lives by inviting death into their blood, God killed an animal. The skins were used as their new covering, which symbolizes that blood must cover death. This first picture of the work of Jesus Christ on the cross shows that God is active in pursuing justice.

Although Jesus had not died on the cross, producing perfect release from sin, God cared about Abel. He heard the sound of his blood and pronounced judgment about Cain. At the same time, he still cared about Cain and pronounced judgment upon *anyone* who would kill him. No matter what the position, the murderer or the murdered, God cares for the lives of both.

To clarify, we are not saying that people should embrace a lawless society where everyone can do whatever they want because of the cross. God created consequences. But our *why* must be substantiated by Jesus. As Christians, our intent in the pursuit of justice for what *we* have suffered at the hands of others must be different than the motivation and aim of unbelievers.

The Purpose of Civil Consequences

If someone is hurting people unreservedly, we who know what is right must intervene, for their sake and the sake of the community. Consequences are executed to protect the community, provide restitution where possible and allow an opportunity for repentance—where someone who is working against the wholeness of the community can turn from their ways and work towards reconciliation. With a Cross-centered perspective, we become greater advocates of justice by not letting the little things slide because we see how even small things contribute to the overall brokenness and division in our communities.

Do we *really* believe that God has the best solutions and that they are worth pursuing? Have our faith leaders taught us to believe God will tell us his solutions if we ask in prayer? Finally, are we willing to live each day as Jesus did, doing only what we see God doing, saying only what we hear God say?

I (Chris) received my college degree in Criminal Justice, and I have continued to think deeply about this topic. While we ought to pursue justice reform and seek to protect the defenseless and speak against oppressors, how we go about it must be informed by the spiritual story we are in. When we are advocating for justice reform, we should advocate for changes in a way and manner that reveals the goodness of God that leads people to repentance. When we vote for leaders who are going to make policies about education, economics, and foreign policy, we need their policies to reveal the goodness of God. And that goodness isn't just that he loved and died for them on the cross, but also that he has a way of living that is better for them. Therefore, we must embrace policies and ideas that align with the ways God has called us to live. Voting for someone who is kind and gentle but advocates for policies that clearly contradict

God's truth is not advancing and revealing the goodness of God. Jesus overthrew the money-changers tables in the temple and called the Pharisees a brood of vipers and children of Satan. The loving and godly thing to do is not always kind in the eyes of men.

This is why, to bring us full circle, our first step towards pursuing justice on this earth must be sincere repentance and surrender to God. Only God knows which broken and flawed candidate has a heart he can use. Only God knows the dramatic solutions we need to reform our criminal justice, and how to implement them in a way that doesn't cause an equal or more considerable amount of harm. Only God knows how to root out the corrupt elements in our nation that are under the power of evil. This evil blinds the minds of those in power and traps them with ideas and values that are opposed to the truth of the gospel and the benefit of God's ways. The Bible says that the minds of all unbelievers are blinded. We would be incredibly ignorant to think that people who don't know God will have better solutions for the ills that plague our society than the Body of Christ.

To be problem-solvers, we have to come before the Lord in humility and pray something like this:

"Lord, I see the symptoms of sin and injustice. I see what I think the problem is, but I am not infallible. Show me what you see. Show me what grieves your heart with what is going on. Bring me face to face and heart to heart with you. I take off all the limits in my life, whatever I've held back from you, I'm giving you access. Whatever I need to unlearn, reveal it. Give me the humility to admit I was wrong. Whatever I have not believed that you need me to believe, reveal it, and give me the humility and grace to accept it. Help me make this not about me being right, but about me working with you to see your goodness revealed to this lost and dying world. Give me the humility to know that I need my fellow believers of every ethnicity and generation. Whatever my bent is, whatever piece of this fight is mine, help me remember that it may not be everyone's, and that's okay. Being different doesn't mean we are enemies. Your ways are higher than our ways, your thoughts than our thoughts.[23] Reveal to me what you are calling me to do, who you are calling me to do it with, when you are calling me to do it, and how you want me to do it."

There are no laws that *tell* people to break the law, so at a certain level, the problem isn't with the legal structure or the system. The problem is with the heart of people who are not living up to the laws that the system has already put in place, e.g., George Floyd's killer. The policeman wasn't living up to the laws that the system has already put into place.

For our society to function, we need the police to be able to question people, and we need people to be *honest*. A police officer needs to be self-aware enough and have enough integrity to admit any fears or prejudices that they have or that the job has developed within them. Continued stress in conflict situations affects everyone. Human coping mechanisms and triggers begin subtly. Law enforcement must have a support system that can coach

---

[23] Isaiah 55:8-9 For my thoughts are not your thoughts, neither are your ways my ways, declares the Lord. For as the heavens are higher than the earth, so are my wyas higher than your ways and my thoughts than your thoughts. (ESV)

and counsel them. Citizen review boards and reporting systems could be implemented so that public servants know that transparency and accountability is part of the job. Words and promises are not enough. Visible follow-through must be required.

Everyone gets triggered. Black males, whether they are guilty of a crime or not, *must* be expected to be triggered when law enforcement is around. That trigger cannot become a reason to remove the consequence of breaking the law if they hurt a police officer; however, the consequence must be weighted appropriately.

As Christians, we must remember that God can heal a person from triggers. Jesus came to destroy all the works of the enemy, including the psychological effects of trauma. Triggers. Unhealthy coping mechanisms. Addictive disorders. Christians are called by God to be ministers of power and healing. Professional counseling has a part to play, but so does Christian ministry. The Body of Christ needs to become more proactive and vocal about the power and mission of Jesus Christ.

Questions:
- What can we do to make sure people who believe they are "above the law" and never get prosecuted or investigated, are held to a godly standard for civil consequences?

- Are there changes you would like to see happen with law enforcement? What are they?

- Is there a scriptural equivalent to modern-day law enforcement? If so, what accountability were they under?

God's Perspective Overrides All

I've (Chris) been hearing people say that the church needs to be front and center in terms of protests, but when I look at the gospels, I see Jesus showing up at the scene, but his approach to governmental reform is different. He doesn't tear down every oppressive system around him in a tangible way. What we see him do is preach the gospel of the Kingdom. We don't always know exactly what Jesus said every time he taught. But we know that since he tells people who have been victimized to love their enemies, bless those who curse them, do good to those who despitefully use, examine the motives of their own heart thoroughly before examining the motives of the other (even in cases of legitimate hurt), *then they have the ability to do so, despite their hurt.*

He addresses oppressive systems by making a point in a nonthreatening manner. For example, he doesn't tear down the entire tax collecting system but reminds them of a higher law. By telling Mary Magdalene to go give the disciples a message, he communicates to these male disciples that he is releasing women from the position that their culture had implemented. In that culture at that time, the words of women were never taken seriously. Jesus' encounter with Mary elevated women to equal standing and authority in Jesus Christ. When dealing with oppressive systems, the only time we see Jesus *lose it* is when he overturned the tables in the temple. His action was appropriate; after all, Jesus is God, and they had their property in the wrong place. The temple was *God's* house.

Jesus showed us how to live submitted to God. He *only* did what God told him he was supposed to do, even at the expense of addressing things that he would have known aren't in alignment with God's highest will. Jesus' priority was to go to the cross. Changing systems wouldn't matter unless he died on the cross, because the biggest issue in the world is, are people freed from the bondage of sin or not?

The cross humbles and challenges all of us, as we remember times in our lives when we have been both oppressor and oppressed in need of the grace, mercy, and healing of God. No longer do we look at another person with anger and rage in our hearts, wondering *how* they could do such a thing, but with pity and compassion as we recognize that we too could end up in their shoes if separated from the life of God and his lavish grace and mercy. We neither condemn nor label people for their actions *because* Christ has freed us from being condemned and labeled from our own. Our pursuit of justice is because we have known and received lavish grace and mercy and want others to partake with us. Our faith journey is supposed to mature us to pursue justice not from a place of woundedness and hurt, but out of compassion and wisdom. We seek the healing of the oppressed equally with the healing of the oppressor, because justice, seen through the cross, reveals a way forward for both.

We tend to focus on what we see, the external and the physical, vs. what we cannot see, the unseen realm of the heart, and the demonic realm. So again, as we peruse the Bible, we find that God doesn't see skin color, our biology, the economic station first; he sees the condition of the heart.

6

Our Way Forward

Voices must be heard. The blood of the slain cries up from the ground. Numerous Old Testament verses talk about the cry of the hurting coming to the ears of God. For my son and me, the cry comes from victims of racial profiling, abortion, neglect in nursing homes, etc. Our Christian goal of healing, unity, and reconciliation must consider the process—the steps that God encourages. In this last chapter, we will list various action points and their implications.

The solutions to the issues of injustice that are present in our modern society are not necessarily going to be found specifically in Scripture. They will be revealed to those seeking the wisdom of the Holy Spirit and those solutions applicable to our time will always be in line with the principles revealed in Scripture.

*****

Some believers may not know what to think about the public outcry that escalated in May after another black man was killed at the hands of law enforcement. Many of these brothers and sisters have watched scenes of people of color marching, chanting, and protesting and resented the display of anger and dismantling of what for them was a peaceful existence. But we read earlier in Genesis 4:10, God's response to injustice is one of dismay. "He said, "What have you done? The voice of your brother's blood is crying to Me from the ground." If the blood-cry of those innocently slain can be heard, how much more the voice of those oppressed due to the color of their skin? The following Scriptures also express God's mind toward justice for the oppressed.

> *God has taken his place in the divine council; in the midst of the gods, he holds judgment: "How long will you judge unjustly and show partiality to the wicked? Selah Give justice to the weak and the fatherless; maintain the right of the afflicted and the destitute. Rescue the weak and the needy; deliver them from the hand of the wicked."* [24]

> *"He has told you, O man, what is good; and what does the Lord require of you but to do justice, and to love kindness, and to walk humbly with your God?"*[25]

---

[24] Psalm 82:1-4 (ESV)

[25] Micah 6:8 (ESV)

Being just is foundational to the nature of God, and all created beings are expected to live just lives. Hopefully, you can see that what God considers just is not always in vogue within our chosen social circles. As people who have committed to following God and embracing his standards of justice, what can we do when we live among people who do not ascribe to Christ's standards?

Allow me (Chris) to provide four guiding principles in how we can practice and pursue justice practically even as we live in a world that is often hostile and in rebellion to God's kingdom and ways.

1. Participate in The Political Process

Participation will look different for all of us. Some God will call to take part by actually serving in government, whether at the local or national level. If that's you, do so as a Christian, a redeemed son or daughter of God who happens to be a political leader. Don't be a political leader, who just happens to be a Christian. The misinterpretation of 'separation of church and state' has led some to believe that our Christian beliefs are personal, but when we enter politics, we have to leave them at the door. That is absolutely in contradiction to a belief that God is the ultimate authority over the earth and all aspects of Creation. We should, as guided by the wisdom of the Holy Spirit and laws of our nation, bring flourishing, restoration, peace, and joy to all we serve in our position of leadership. We do those people a disservice by not advocating for policies and principles that align for God's highest good for people.

In addition, if you are participating in the political process with your vote, we must make sure that our candidates, as much as they are able, follow and uphold a biblical standard of morality and justice. (I would recommend Deuteronomy 13-26 as a great starting place to develop a solid biblical foundation by which to evaluate platforms of those running for elected office).

Lastly, make sure that the way and manner in which you participate in the political process is an accurate representation of the new life we have in Christ. If Christians can't have a civil conversation about difficult issues and policies, what sort of witness is that to the nature and character of God for those he desires to reach with his love?

2. Pray for ALL People And ALL In Authority

First of all, then, I urge that supplications, prayers, intercessions, and thanksgivings be made for all people, for kings and all who are in high positions, that we may lead a peaceful and quiet life, godly and dignified in every way. This is good, and it is pleasing in the sight of God our Savior, who desires all people to be saved and to come to the knowledge of the truth. For there is one God, and there is one mediator between God and men, the man Christ Jesus, who gave himself as a ransom for all, which is the testimony given at the proper time. [26]

---

[26] 1 Timothy 2:1-6 (ESV)

Paul says that he desires that all lead a peaceful and quiet life, godly, and dignified in every way. And the path to that kind of life, he says, begins with daily prayer for all people, leaders or otherwise. If we see unjust activity in our communities, we need first to assess our prayer discipline. Does our prayer life resemble what Paul says is necessary for *all* to lead a peaceful and quiet life? Or do we regularly focus on our own needs? Are we praying for God to shower our leaders with wisdom and protect them from spiritual attack? Are we praying out of honor or out of accusation, judgment, or even jealousy? Are we praying blessings over our leaders, or speaking curses under the guise of 'venting'? Remember, we live in the middle of a spiritual battle, and the example of scripture reveals that political leaders often experience that battle at a greater level of intensity. Let's be part of the solution and not part of the problem.

3. Invest in Your Immediate Community

This is what the Lord of Heaven's Armies, the God of Israel, says to all the captives he has exiled to Babylon from Jerusalem: "Build homes, and plan to stay. Plant gardens and eat the food they produce. Marry and have children. Then find spouses for them so that you may have many grandchildren. Multiply! Do not dwindle away! ***And work for the peace and prosperity of the city where I sent you into exile. Pray to the***

Lord for it, for its welfare will determine your welfare." Jeremiah 29:4-7 NLT [emphasis mine]

The implications of this passage are staggering. The Jewish people have undergone judgment for rebellion against God for generations. The nations of Assyria, and most recently, Babylon, have conquered the people, and they've been carried away into exile. AND YET, on the other side of judgment, exiled to live as second-class citizens in a pagan land that worships false gods, God calls his people to live with *intentionality*, as they still represent him as his chosen people. Within this passage are four principles that we can adopt.

"Build homes and plan to stay." What would it look like for you to view where you live not as a place chosen based on comfort, its entertainment options, its school systems, or nightlife, but instead as a place you've been sent to on a long-term assignment in order to see it transformed and restored to the glory of God? In a time when the world is smaller than ever, and it's so easy to embrace a transitory lifestyle, I believe that those who plant roots and are willing to make the sacrifice to invest in a community for 10, 15, or even 20 years will be the ones who have enough skin in the game to see God's justice and restoration transform their communities. Why? Because communities are made up of people, it takes time to develop the trust necessary to ask people to embrace change when they are comfortable with the status quo. As the saying goes, people only care how much you know when they know how much you care.

"Plant gardens and eat the fruit they produce." I'll admit, I don't have a green thumb. Fortunately, I don't believe we have to apply this statement literally, although we ought to consider it! No, I believe the spirit behind this is calling us to see our work differently. So often, we view our work as a necessary evil to make enough money to provide for our chosen lifestyle. I believe God is calling us to reframe our thinking, and instead view ourselves in our workplaces as farmers and gardeners. Gardeners understand the times and the seasons. They understand what they can and cannot control. They embrace a life of faith and faithfulness in the process. They are committed to flourishing and fruitfulness. They work to produce an abundance so that they can live generously to those around them. I don't know what this will look like for you in your specific occupation, but encourage you to pray about these ideas, trusting the Holy Spirit to lead you into all truth.

"Marry and have children...Multiply! Do not dwindle away!" I believe God is restoring his plan and purpose for the institution of the family these days. For many of us, our views of marriage and family are more based on society, culture, and our personal experience than God's revealed intent in scripture. Hear me clearly, I am single and in my twenties, but I recognize that marriage is not primarily about falling in love and being happy. Nor are children to be viewed as burdens who take up our free time and limit our opportunities, so we should strategically plan for when they show up. Neither is the concept of family meant to be limited to those you are biologically related to. Marriage, like all things, is a calling from God, meant to be embraced within the concept of his larger plan for our lives and this world. When God created humanity, he didn't create a full community. He created the institution of marriage and revealed that it was through that covenantal bond that his rule and reign on the earth was to spread across the earth through families (Gen. 1:26-28). Family, I believe, is meant to be one of the primary vehicles of kingdom expansion and renewal in these times. If you are called to marriage, view your marriage, and any children you may have as an opportunity to model a community and society that lives out the principles of God's kingdom. Christian families ought to be the standard of wholeness and lead the way in raising children who embody God's heart for justice. For all, invest in the family of God. We need spiritual fathers and mothers who are willing to 'adopt' the fatherless and motherless in their communities; accepting them before their behavior changes, teaching them about the true sonship available to those who in Christ, modeling what it looks like to commit to love when it is hard, displaying to them the joy of living a life of joyful intentionality rooted in living from our God-given identity and towards our God designated purpose. Embracing our role in the family of God, and actually living a Christ-following life in community with others, is a powerful way to work towards establishing God's justice in our neighborhoods, cities, states, and ultimately, our nations.

"Work for the Peace and Prosperity of the city...Pray to the Lord for it, for its welfare will determine your welfare." What a sobering thought. The welfare of our immediate community will determine our welfare. So, let's commit ourselves to embracing the life of the justice-loving God within us, praying daily, working faithfully, loving generously, and serving sacrificially.

4. Be the Good Samaritan

Be a good Samaritan who treats all in need as their neighbor regardless of ethnicity, religion, sex, political affiliation, income level, appearance, age, or criminal record.

Read Luke 10:25-37 and put yourself in the story, first as the Jewish man. In his place, who are those who ought to help you but don't? Who is the Samaritan in your story, the one you despise, the person who holds the opinions you cannot stand on social media? Now flip the story. If you were the Samaritan, who has scorned you, treating you as a second-class citizen, thumbing their nose at you at every turn. If they were hurt, and you knew who they were and what they believed, would you help them, or pass by?

Would you mow their lawn? Would you buy their groceries? Would you visit them at the hospital? Would you watch their kids? Would you invite them to the barbecue? Would you *love* them? Pursuing justice as God does will inevitably lead to us having to love the unlovable, our enemies, or those that consider us enemies. It is here that our heart for justice is truly tested. It is here that the cross confronts our pursuit of justice. How will you respond?

Civil Rights Today

It gives people false hope to affirm their belief that individual and corporate healing can come through protests, solidarity, and honest dialogue. These provide neighborly comfort—people of color wrap their arms around each other, weep and say, "No justice, no peace." Some are satisfied when white people unite with the cause by acknowledging their privilege or finally learning about the darker side of American history. The marches and dialogue offer an emotional release for sure. But these are band-aids for a deeper wound that is being ignored.

The civil rights movement was rooted in the black church and shepherded by faith leaders, but today is a different day. The 1960s movement was faith-based. Today's movement is mainly secular. Christ-centered voices for civil rights are usually unreported by mainstream media. Also, times have changed in the black community. We cannot automatically associate black people with Christianity or "the church." Doing so is an insult to many black people who find Christianity or the Bible contrary to their prescribed worldview.

As Christians, we must enter civil conversations wisely and humbly. We cannot assume that our inherited or denominational views and values are God-approved. *This* was the error of Christian slave owners, who translated the Bible through a lens of domination. We must study the significance of the cross, redemption, forgiveness, inherited sin, loving your enemy, being a new creation in Christ, and other relevant topics. These must be grappled with and resolved in our hearts. We need to keep the Word before our eyes when we protest, post on social media, or watch the news. Conversations and civil engagement in the public square must occur, remembering that God sees two groups, not groups based on skin color or political ideology, but based on the kingdom in which they belong.

If you are born again, do what the Holy Spirit leads you to do when injustices occur, not what guilt or fear of man urges you to do, and not what your friend or the media tells you to do.

Our Mouth and James 3

Daily we must ask ourselves, Have I surrendered my tongue and words to the Lordship of Christ? We want to speak from a place of grace, mercy, and purity, not returning evil for evil, but returning evil with good. What do the words we speak about those who have hurt us or those we care about reflect: one who is still living from the wound, or someone who has allowed Christ to heal the wound?

Economic Justice

Equity and fairness are common terms in the mission for social justice. Although we are still studying the Bible to align our mindset with God's concerning the terms equity and fairness, I (Tina) will share several scriptures that have come up. The main questions we are trying to answer right now are: How does God present his perspective on economics, financial stewardship, lack, and gain in the Bible? Does God care about fairness the way we do? What scriptures answer this question for us?

Whether economic, educational, or health care access, in general, equity is the mission to give everyone an even playing field, the same terms, and ideally the same outcome of success. First, let's start by realizing that God cares about people's economic success. He encourages giving (Proverbs 22:9) and helping those that lack (Deut. 24:19-20). Many verses describe God as a lavish (Isaiah 25:6) and a generous Father (Matt 20:15). If we are to reflect Him, we will be the same (Proverbs 11:25). In fact, Deut. 15 is the passage that gives instructions for the year of Sabbath, which involves remitting debt, generous giving to those who lack and release from bond service.

Does God give each human being the same opportunities at birth, or is he like the master in Matt 25:14-29, who wants to see what we do with what we are given, whether it is much or little? As we read this passage and others, we try to discover God's perspective on "fair." He sovereignly chooses which family and country we are born into. Would we call this fair? Or He is focused on the purposes that we are individually called to carry out? Consider the boy born into a wealthy family that has rejected God, and a boy born to a poor single mother who loves Jesus. The first is born into a spiritually lacking situation. The latter is born into an economically lacking situation. Is this fair?

Let's look at the parable where Jesus told about the talents In Matthew 25: 14-29. A talent was a quantity of money, determined by weight. Jesus told parables to give listeners a view of God's Kingdom ways. In this parable, the man in charge, or boss gives each of his servants a different number of talents, "each one according to his own ability." As a result of their individual abilities, they received a different amount of money and were charged to steward it in the way he would approve. When we get to the end of the passage, we find out that the servant who received the least number of talents hid them due to fear and his view of his boss's integrity. He received a huge rebuke. His boss told him that he didn't invest the talent wisely. So, the boss took the money back and gave it to the one who had the most talents. Jesus concludes the parable with a principle. "For to everyone who has, more shall be given, and he will have an abundance, but from the one who does not have, even what he does have shall be taken away." Was this "fair"?

As we think about economic injustice, financial stewardship, and our response to those who lack, two other scriptural principles come to mind: the law of sowing and reaping and the law of giving. Both verses suggest that in God's kingdom, those that sow in good ground will always have more than those that do not. This seems different from the current mission of economic justice, which has the goal of everyone having not only an equal opportunity but *an equal outcome*.

Sowing and reaping can be positive or negative and do not always have to do with economics. Proverbs 22:8 says, "He who sows iniquity will reap vanity." The point is that whether economics or sin, there is a return-on-investment principle. Similar is the principle found in Luke 6:38. I (Tina) have heard this verse applied to monetary giving or offerings, but the concept of sowing and reaping applies.

Give, and it will be given to you. They will pour into your lap a good measure—pressed down, shaken together, and running over. For by your standard of measure it will be measured to you in return.

The phrase "running over" suggests abundance for those who are beneficent with whatever they are giving. Lastly, in Mark 12:41-44, Jesus tells the disciples his perspective of giving and economic class. The scene involves Jesus and his disciples sitting outside the treasury. We don't know what the disciples were doing, but Jesus was observing the different people who came to deposit their money. The rich have a lot to deposit, but a poor widow catches his attention. She puts in two small coins. Jesus gets his disciples attention and tells them, "This poor widow put in more than all the contributors to the treasury; for they all put in out of their surplus, but she, out of her poverty, put in all she owned, all she had to live on."

Interestingly, Jesus doesn't *ridicule* rich people for what they have. He doesn't teach the disciples a principle that they should be made to give their surplus to the widow. We already know his view on generosity. He would rather that giving come from a sincere and glad heart than an obligation (Colossians 3:23).

What type of goal is appropriate when it comes to economic justice if biblical economics deals with faithful stewardship of resources no matter how large or small, the generosity of people, and the challenge of sinful mindsets? As we have discussed in this book, injustice is rooted in the human heart and then permeates systems.

Only a revelation of the lovingkindness of God can soften and redeem the human heart. Although systemic injustice is a reality because broken people govern systems, episodes of inequality do not mean that the system is doing something wrong. If the servant who had been given one talent had used this talent, invested it, sowed it to the best of the abilities he had, he would have experienced gain and promotion.

Marketable Phrases and The Bible

What is wrong with being *color blind*? As a young person, I (Tina) was gripped by the words of Dr. Martin Luther King, who encouraged people to be known for their character and not their skin color. Once, as a teen, I saw a woman who had been badly burned; the scarring of third-degree burn damage made it impossible to know her ethnicity. She could have been black or white. Witnessing her made a deep impression on me as King's words came to life. We do need to see through the spectrum of skin color and see a person's true essence. Of course, I understand that the current phrase *color blind* is meant to help erase the lack of conscience effort to understand racial injustice. People of color want and need white people to acknowledge racial discrimination. And color blind is a shrewd phrase that expresses this mission. As a Jesus follower, I must recognize, however, that this highly commercial message undercuts the message of Galatians 3:28.

There is neither Jew nor Greek, there is neither slave nor free, there is neither male nor female; for you are all one in Christ Jesus.

In God's eyes, divine distinctions like skin color, biology, economic station, and nationality can be acknowledged, but they are *secondary* to our highest reality when it comes to our identity in Christ.

I know many Christians who are not color-blind, yet they do not use *skin color* as a factor in their interactions. These brothers and sisters reflect Jesus' manner with others and produce the fruit of a renewed mind. While our lighter-skinned brothers and sisters understand the reality of the phrase *white privilege*, they should not be accused of racial desensitization just because they don't focus on skin color. As redeemed citizens of heaven, white Jesus-followers should repel *white guilt,* not embrace it. Maybe your great-great-grandfather did own my great-great-grandfather. Generational freedom comes when you renounce his deeds as sin, ask God to cleanse your bloodline from the iniquity of his sin, and then ask Him to cancel the spiritual and natural consequences of that sin. After that, go in the peace of the Lord Jesus Christ! Shame is the devil's quicksand. So are guilt and fear.

Whoever coined this phrase was clever; however, white *guilt* is as sinful and destructive as black *pride*. Both guilt and pride are self-destructive. Words, even clever phrases, are too powerful in God's creative reality to be used with a limited understanding of what they produce.

Do a word study on "words," and you will discover why God urges us to be slow to speak, and why He says death and life are in the power of the tongue. God has given humanity a degree of creative ability. What we say produces something—an effect. We all have heard of verbal abuse. Words undermine not just individual destiny but corporate heath. So, when we agree with or embrace cultural guilt or pride, we are destroying the abundant life Christ bought for us and the fruit of forgiveness and humility. White people should never embrace guilt. Black people should never embrace pride. Our lesson should be to choose our words wisely. Or, as my husband says to our children, "Say what you mean, not what sounds cool" (or marketable).

How To Protest
To another fellow Christian, I say, "Jesus has been weeping with you and your family for generations. Only he can wipe your tears away. You've grown up with a target on your back. Cast your cares on Him. Give him your anger and fear because it's too heavy for any human to bear. Remind yourself that you are seated with Him in heavenly places, far above all principality and power, and ask Him to teach you how to use *his* weapons to defeat demonic systems and wicked strategies. Protesting is not wrong! But it is ineffectual if Jesus is not front and center.

Spiritual Factors - The Devil
We must also remember that the battle we are in is, in reality, a battle about a King and his kingdom. We cannot separate our pursuit of justice from the rule and reign of God that Scripture reveals is consistently being opposed by rebellious spiritual forces. While we get a glimpse of

this conflict about the destinies of nations in Daniel 10, Paul reminds us in Ephesians 2 that the enemy is consistently at work to blind the minds of unbelievers to the goodness and grace of God, lest they repent and embrace Him as Lord and King of their lives. In addition, after painting a picture of healthy relational dynamics within different groups within the church at that time: husbands and wives, parents and children, and masters and slaves; the Apostle Paul writes this:

"A final word: Be strong in the Lord and his mighty power. Put on all of God's armor so that you will be able to stand firm against all strategies of the devil. For we are not fighting against flesh-and-blood enemies, but against evil rulers and authorities of the unseen world, against mighty powers in this dark world, and evil spirits in the heavenly places."[27]

As we work to live out the truths revealed in Scripture, we are going to experience conflict. It is inevitable. But it is *so* important that we rightly discern the root of the conflict. In these verses, Paul calls Christians to realize that any relational conflict we experience, whether it's family conflict or racism, has its roots in what is going on in the *unseen* world. As Christians, we are to recognize that this is where our real enemy resides. Our enemy is not a Republican or a Democrat. Our enemy is not the Alt-Right or the progressive left. Our enemy is not the immigrant coming across the border or the neighbor who loves his guns too much. Our enemy is the one who seeks to deceive

---

[27] Ephesians 6:10-12 NLT

people—*all people*—causing them to embrace values that lead them to bondage and not freedom. Our enemy is one who encourages accusation and condemnation, not forgiveness and reconciliation. Our enemy is one who fosters self-righteous judgment rather than a humble and loving confrontation. Our enemy is one who seeks to kill, steal, and destroy[28] us by any means necessary, and he and his dark forces try to prevent us from moving forward into life, and life more abundantly.

The devil has been ultimately defeated on the cross, but as the body of Christ, we still play an important role in executing that victory. How we submit to the Holy Spirit and follow Christ in our daily lives determines our effectiveness in establishing God's victory in our lives and communities. Human beings have been given free will. We can choose to align ourselves with the influence and goals of our spiritual enemy. There are real consequences to that.

In our contending, if we make people the focus of our opposition rather than the focus of God's redemption plan, we miss the mark. We are to view others the way God does—as people he wants to redeem and not condemn. Not that humanity is perfect or righteous on our own, but we are of immense value to God, *even* in our sin, *even* when we oppose him. I am worth the life of the very Son of God. If that's true for me, and that's true for you, then it's true for *all*; and we must determine to treat everyone as if they carry that worth to God. We should not excuse their sin or crimes but allow their value before God

---

[28] John 10:10 NKJV

to dictate *how* we respond and bring justice to the situations in which they are involved.

*****

God has given us his Spirit[29] and is sanctifying our lives to make us more like Jesus. As we yield to this transformation, we offer God's life to others by responding as Christ would to social issues. As we renew our minds through the lens of God's Word, our perceptions change, and we will see people, problems, and protests differently. Lastly, when we view people through God's unconditional love and abundant grace, we will be less reactionary and more forgiving. Exchanging a secular mindset for a biblical one leads to Christlike action and response as we all look to represent and reveal God's justice in our neighborhoods, cities, and nation.

<u>Final Questions:</u>

- In the last few years, have there been corporate responses to an injustice that you believe are unbiblical? If so, why?

- How does Jesus tell individuals (versus corporate bodies) to respond to injustice?

- One of the missions of anti-racism is to cause a person to be self-aware of their attitudes and practices that are racist (microaggressions). Can you find biblical support for this mission?

---

[29] Galatian 5:22 For the fruit of the Spirit is love, joy, peace, patience, kindness, goodness, faithfulness, gentleness and self-control.

- Another mission of anti-racism is to hold discriminatory structures accountable and charge them to dismantle procedures and practices that propagate skin-tone bias (racial discrimination). From a sin/Cross point of view to what extent can this mission be carried out?

- What biblical role do Christian authority figures have in shining the light on someone's sinful mindsets that lead to injustice? Compare Jesus' approach to the Romans, the Pharisees, the disciples, and others with whom he spoke.

- In terms of your church congregation or Christian social networks, what type of tangible proof would convince you that their hearts have been purged of skin-color bias? What does Scripture inform you about your answer?

- How can you work for the peace and prosperity of your city?

- Do you believe Ephesians 6:12-18 is literal? Why or why not?

- How does the Bible tell us to deal with a person's sin and deal with demonic spirits that oppress people?

- Based on your last answer, what would you say to police officers that have murdered black males? What would you say to looters? Protestors? Antifa?

- Do you pray daily for those in positions of authority? Why or why not? Do you believe that your prayers are effectual? Why or why not?

- If you are a person of color or a woman who has suffered injustice, could you be a Good Samaritan to a person who represents the group that treated you unjustly? E.g., a police officer officer

- Economic injustice – Read these scriptures: Proverbs 10:4, 13:18, 14:31, 21:13, 22:22, 28:19,35:10. What do you glean from these verses in terms of the causes and remedies for poverty?

- Wealth – Read these scriptures. What do you glean from these verses? Deut. 7:12-14, 8:18, Prov 8:21, 13:11, 13:22, 1 Timothy 6:10, Malachi 3:8-12 What do these verses reveal about stewardship? Lack? Social responsibility? Family inheritance? Work? Considering current opinions about economic injustice, what do the scriptures in this question and the last convey about God's perspective?

Books by Tina Webb

Culture Changers: Understand the Roots of Brokenness and Help Heal Your Family and Community

The climate of present-day America presents anger and fear instead of hope. From hashtag movements to substance abuse increase, the media and statistics reveal that people are hurting. Many of us recognize the declaration of God in this hour: lives must shift. By walking alongside people in their journey towards wholeness, we can be hands that strengthen the weak and voices that unlock vision. By understanding how God created us, spirit, soul, and body, we will confidently help people discover how to overcome the obstacles they face each day. Individual wholeness carries corporate benefits on every level- family and community. **culturechangersbook.com**

Cultivating the Souls of Parents: Facing our Brokenness; Embracing His Likeness

Raising a child helps us discover that parenting involves a whole lot of digging, not just through piles of mismatched socks, but also through layers of insecurities and heart issues that our children and we have. I will never have a place where I can say as a parent, "I have arrived!" No, this process of parenting brings to light my own emotional brokenness that God wants me to explore and bring to Him to remedy and make whole. **tinawebb.net**

Books by Christopher Webb

Signs Along the Road, A Thirty-Day Devotional and Journal
Available October 2020

Remembering. This task takes effort and desire when the truth that must be remembered is more than our day-to-day lists and schedules. God's truths, who you are and who He is must be dwelt upon to 1) pursue God's plan for your life and 2) build a testimony of God's faithfulness to us. Christopher Webb gears our minds and hearts to take note of the signs that God is with us. The devotional includes a formatted guide with questions to help you dedicate thirty days to meditate on the truths in Scripture and make a note of God's present involvement in your life.
thechristopherwebb.wordpress.com

Made in the USA
Monee, IL
15 February 2022

90506419R00059